THE Rhyme Bible Storybook

FOR TODDLERS

BY L.J. SATTGAST

ILLUSTRATED BY TONI GOFFE

Zonderkidz

THE RHYME BIBLE STORYBOOK FOR TODDLERS
Copyright 1999 by L. J. Sattgast
Illustrations by Toni Goffe

ISBN: 0-310-70078-7

Library of Congress Cataloging-in-Publication Data:

Sattgast, L. J., 1953-
The rhyme Bible for toddlers/by L.J. Sattgast; illustrated by Toni Goffe.
    p.   cm.
Summary: A collection of stories from both the Old and New
Testaments, told in simple rhyming text.
ISBN 0-310-70078-7   (alk. Paper)
    1.   Bible stories, English. [1.Bible stories.] I. Goffe, Toni, ill. II. Title.

BS551.2.S366 1999
220.9'505-dc21   99-13144

                                                                            CIP

The Rhyme Bible Storybook for Toddlers was previously published by Gold
and Honey, a division of Multnomah Publishers

Zonderkidz™
The children's group of Zondervan

Printed in the United States of America
    02 03 04 / RRD-C / 7 6

CONTENTS

NEW TESTAMENT

OLD TESTAMENT

God Made Everything

GENESIS 1 & 2

In the beginning,
God made the light.
The light was for day,
The dark was for night.

God made the sky,
And God made the sea.
He made every plant
And flower and tree.

God made the sun,
So shiny and bright;
The moon and the stars
That glow at night.

Then He made animals—
Oh, what fun!
God must have smiled
When He made each one!

God made a man
And a woman too.
Then God rested
Because He was through.

The Floating Zoo

GENESIS 6–9

God told Noah
To build a boat,
So Noah is making
A boat that will float.

What will he put
In his great big boat?
Tigers and elephants,
Camels and goats!

Lions and zebras
Are safe inside.
Monkeys and hippos
Are ready to ride.

Down comes the rain,
And up goes the boat.
Noah is glad
To see it can float!

It rains and it rains,
And it rains some more.
But then the rain stops,
And down goes the door.

Out they scamper—
Jump, skip, hop!
Everyone's glad
To see the rain stop!

The Promise

Abraham and Sarah
Had camels to ride.
They traveled together,
Side by side.

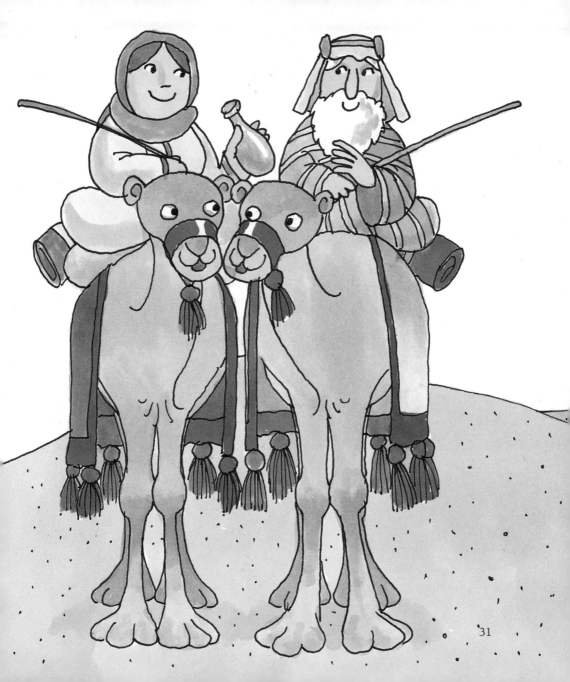

31

They had lots of goats.
They had lots of sheep.
Shhhhhhh!
Better be quiet,
They're all fast asleep!

But Abraham and Sarah
Didn't have a son,
Though God had promised
To give them one.

They waited and waited.
They hoped and they prayed.
Would God really keep
The promise He made?

God kept His promise—
He gave them a boy
Who filled their hearts
With laughter and joy!

Joseph Forgives

GENESIS 37–46

Joseph is getting
A present from Dad.
It makes his brothers
Jealous and mad.

41

They grab his beautiful
Coat one day
And send poor Joseph
Far, far away.

But Joseph works hard
In everything,
So God makes him helper
To Pharaoh the king.

When Joseph's brothers
Come into town,
What will he do
When they all bow down?

Joseph hugs them
One by one
And says, "I forgive you
For what you have done!"

49

Baby in a Boat

EXODUS 2

"Hush, little baby.
Don't make a noise.
Pharaoh's soldiers
Don't like little boys."

"Now, little baby,
I've made you a boat.
I'll put you inside
And set you afloat."

But Pharaoh's daughter
Saw it nearby,
And when she looked
He started to cry.

The baby's big sister
Ran for their mother.
She went to get help
For her baby brother.

Then Pharaoh's daughter
Opened her purse
And paid the baby's mother
To be his nurse!

59

God Helps Us

EXODUS 2–15

Why won't Pharaoh
Let us go?
When we ask him
He says NO!

But God sends frogs
To hop around,
And God puts locusts
On the ground.

God sends swarms
Of buzzing flies,
And see how dark
He makes the skies!

Pharaoh finally
Sets us free.
Then God helps us
Cross the sea.

How the people
Dance and sing,
"Thank you, God,
For everything!"

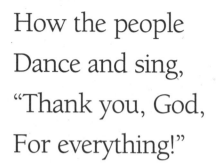

The Wall Falls

JOSHUA 1–6

Look at this wall.
It's big and tall.
But *we're* not big,
And *we're* not tall.
We can't climb
This great big wall.

But we can march
And not say a word.
Only our trumpets
Can be heard.

One last time
The trumpet blows,
And when it blows
Then everyone knows...

75

It's time to make
A great, big sound—
Everyone SHOUTS
And the wall falls down!

Ruth Is Kind

BOOK OF RUTH

A girl named Ruth
Was kind and good.
She helped Naomi
Whenever she could.

"What shall we eat?"
Naomi said.
"We need some grain
To make our bread."

"I can help,"
Ruth gladly said.
"I'll find grain
To make our bread."

Ruth worked hard.
She didn't complain.
So Boaz gave her
Lots of grain.

God gave Ruth
A family,
And they all lived
Quite happily!

Samuel Listens

I SAMUEL 1–3

Samuel, Samuel,
What do you hear?
"I hear Eli
Coming near."

Here is Eli,
Old and gray.
Samuel obeys him
Day after day.

Samuel, Samuel,
What do you hear?
"I hear God,
And He is near."

Samuel listens,
And Samuel is right!
For God has something
To say tonight.

Even when Samuel
Grows old and gray,
He listens when God
Has something to say!

97

David and Goliath

I SAMUEL 17

Goliath was a giant,
A great BIG giant!
He stood as tall as a tree.
"HA! HA! HA!"
Goliath would laugh,
"Everyone's afraid of me!"

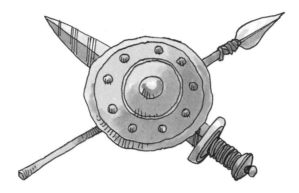

Goliath had a spear,

A long, sharp spear.

He carried a shield and sword.

David was a boy,

A very young boy,

Who said, "I trust in the Lord!"

David had a sling
And five smooth stones.
The sling went around and around.
Whizzz! went the stone
As it flew through the air,
And the giant came tumbling down!

103

Where Did Jonah Go?

BOOK OF JONAH

God spoke to Jonah.
He said, "Go! Go! Go!"
But Jonah didn't listen.
He said, "No! No! No!"

Jonah ran and tried to hide.
He found a ship and went inside.
But God sent stormy winds outside
To blow, blow, blow!

Jonah told the sailors,
"You should throw, throw, throw.
Throw me out, and then the storm
Will go, go, go."

But swimming in the deep blue sea,
A fish was waiting hungrily.
It swallowed Jonah easily—
Oh! Oh! Oh!

Jonah prayed inside the fish,
So, so sad.
He said to God, "I'm sorry
I was so, so bad."

The fish threw Jonah on the sand,
And Jonah heard the Lord's command:
"Go and preach in other lands,
Go! Go! Go!"

And Jonah said,
(Can you guess?)
"Yes! Yes! Yes!"

117

Daniel Prays

Daniel prayed in the morning,
And Daniel prayed at night.
Daniel prayed when he ate his lunch,
For he knew that this was right.

Then some men
Said a terrible thing:
"Don't pray to God—
Pray to the KING!"

But Daniel said
As he knelt to pray,
"GOD is the one
I must obey!"

123

The men told the king,
And what happened then?
Daniel was thrown
In the lions' den!

The hungry lions licked their chops,
But something made the lions stop.
An angel shut their mouths so tight
They didn't get a single bite!

NEW TESTAMENT

Who Saw Jesus?

LUKE 2

Little baby Jesus
Lying on the hay,
Who was there to see Him
On that first Christmas Day?

131

Mary was His mother.

She held Him in her arms.

She wrapped Him up

In strips of cloth

To keep Him safe and warm.

Gentle Joseph saw Him.
He smiled at Him and said,
"You'll need a place
Where You can sleep,
So here's a manger bed."

The holy angels saw Him
And sang a song of joy!
They told some shepherds
Where to find
This very special boy.

137

The shepherds ran to see Him.
They knelt and bowed their heads,
For Jesus was the Son of God
Upon a manger bed.

Where Is Jesus?

LUKE 2

"Jesus is missing.
Where could He be?
We'll ask our friends
And our family."

"Have you seen Jesus?"
"He isn't with me!"
"Where, oh where
Could Jesus be?"

So back they went
The way they came.
And all the way back
They called out His name.

They looked for His face
In the marketplace.
They looked up and down
The streets of the town.

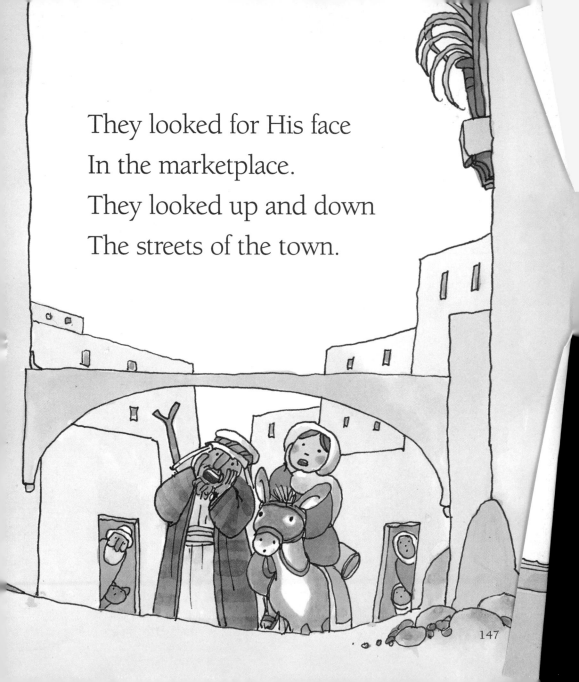

147

At last they went
To the Temple to look,
And there was Jesus—
Reading God's Book!

John the Baptist

What did John the Baptist wear?
He wore a coat of camel hair.
What did John the Baptist eat?
Locusts and honey—what a treat!

What did John the Baptist say?
"Someone is coming
To show you the way."
What did John the Baptist do?
He baptized the people,
Then Jesus came too.

But when God said,

"This is My Son!"

John the Baptist's work was done.

What did John the Baptist say?

"Follow Jesus—

He'll show you the way!"

155

A Wish for Fish

LUKE 5

We fish and fish
And wish and wish.
How we wish
We'd catch some fish!

We fished all night
And now we're done.
We didn't catch
A single one!

Then Jesus says,
"Listen to Me.
Throw your nets
Into the sea!"

"We already tried
To catch some fish,
But we will do it
If You wish!"

Jesus helps us
Get our wish.
Our net is full
Of wiggly fish!

165

"Follow Me,"
Says Jesus then.
"I will help you
Fish for men!"

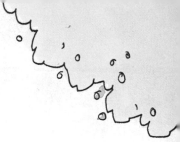

A Tasty Lunch

JOHN 6

Out on a hillside
Next to the beach,
The people listened
To Jesus preach.

169

But dinnertime came,
And rumble, rumble, rumble,
The people could hear
Their stomachs grumble!

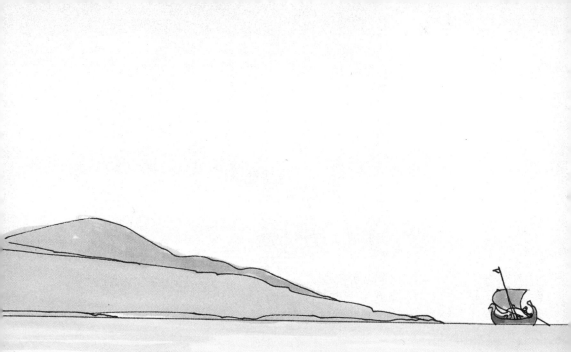

"What shall we feed them?"
Philip said.
"We don't have the money
To buy enough bread!"

173

But one little boy
Had fish and bread.
It made Jesus smile.
"That's plenty!" He said.

While all of the people
Sat on the ground,
He blessed the boy's lunch
And passed it around.

"Mmmmm," said the people.
"Munch, munch, munch!"
Jesus fed them all
With one little lunch!

The Happy Dad

A sick little girl
Was lying in bed.
"What can I do?"
Her daddy said.

Then he remembered
That Jesus was near.
"Good!" said her dad,
"I'll bring Jesus here!"

Jesus was happy
To go with the dad.
He told the dad,
"Now don't be sad!"

186

When Jesus came
To the daddy's place,
He smiled and looked
At the little girl's face.

"Get up!" Jesus said,
And the daddy could tell
That his dear little girl
Was happy and well!

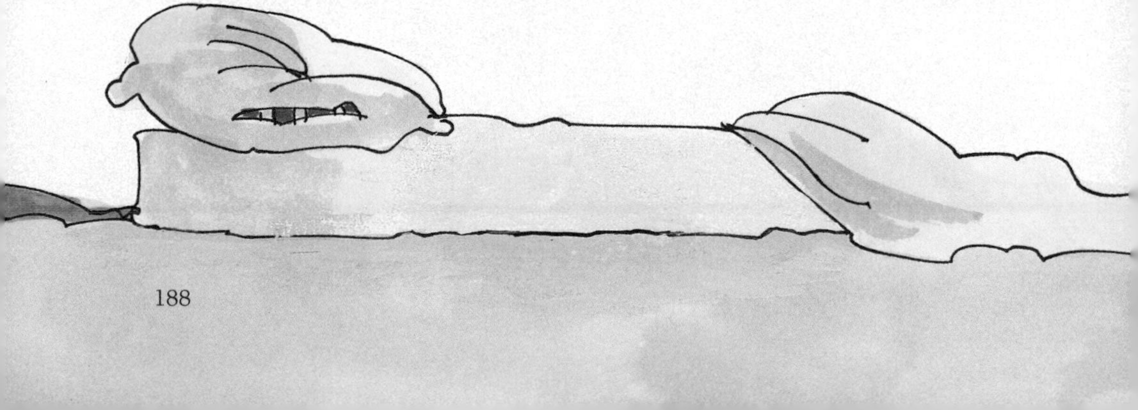

189

The Farmer

A Story Jesus Told

MATTHEW 13

A farmer scattered
Seeds one day.
The birds took some
And flew away.

Some seeds fell
On a rocky spot.
They withered and died
When the sun grew hot.

Some seeds fell
Among the weeds.
The weeds grew big
And choked the seeds.

196

But some seeds fell
On ground that was good,
And the plants grew up
Just as they should.

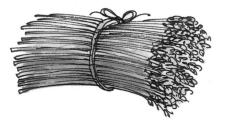

God's Word is like seeds
That grow good deeds!

The Lost Lamb

A Story Jesus Told

LUKE 15

A shepherd has
One hundred sheep.
He counts them all
Before they sleep.

"Ninety-six, ninety-seven,
Ninety-eight, ninety-nine. . .
Uh-oh!
Where's that littlest
Lamb of mine?"

The shepherd searches
Far and near.
"What's that sound
I think I hear?"

204

It's Little Lamb
So cold and wet!
The shepherd says,
"Now don't you fret!"

The shepherd calls
His friends around.
"My lamb was lost
But now it's found!"

Lambs like *you*
Are loved by God too!

Children Come to Jesus

All day long
The people come.
Jesus greets them
One by one.

Short ones, tall ones,
Big ones, small ones.
Happy ones, grumpy ones,
Thin ones, plump ones.

Children come
And say, "Hooray!"
But Jesus' friends
Say, "Go away!"

Jesus tells them,
"Come to Me.
You can sit
Upon My knee!"

Jesus hugs them.
Hear Him pray:
"Bless each child
Who came today!"

The Blind Man

MARK 10

A blind man listened.
What did he hear?
He heard that Jesus
Was coming near.

The blind man cried
Upon his knees,
"Jesus! Jesus!
Help me, please!"
"Shhhh!" said the crowd.
"You're much too loud!"

But Jesus said,
"Bring him to Me."
And Jesus helped
The blind man see!

223

Little Zacchaeus

LUKE 19

Little Zacchaeus
Was much too small.
"Why," he asked,
"Is everyone tall?"

"I'll stand on my toes
And s-t-r-e-t-c-h my nose.
Oh, fiddle-dee-dee!
I *still* can't see!"

"I know what I'll do—
I'll climb up a tree!"
And that's how Zacchaeus
Was able to see.

Jesus came by
And looked in the tree.
"Come down, Zaccheus,
And eat with Me!"

"Jesus, You mean
You'll eat with *me?*"
So happy Zacchaeus
Came down from the tree!

Jesus Is Coming

LUKE 19–23

Jesus is coming
Into the town!
Take off your coats
And lay them down!

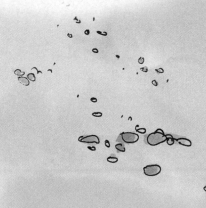

Jesus is coming
Into the town!
Pick up a branch
And wave it around!

Jesus is coming!

Let's all sing:

"Hosanna! Hosanna!

To Jesus the King!"

But Jesus knows
That there are some
Who do not like
To see Him come.

They will hang Him
On a tree,
And He will die
For you and me.

Jesus Is Alive!

JOHN 20

In the garden Mary cried.
She was sad that Jesus died.
"Do not cry," an angel said.
He's alive, He isn't dead!"

When she saw Him
Then she knew
That what the angel
Said was true!

All His friends
Were happy then.
Jesus was alive again!

249

Good-bye

Jesus told His friends one day,
"Pretty soon I'll go away.
Don't be sad at what I say—
I will come again someday!"

Jesus' friends were standing by
When UP He went, into the sky!

Jesus' friends went here and there,

Telling people everywhere,

"Jesus is God's only Son,

And He loves you, every one!"